dark blue is celebrating all
…..
nature colourful

Impressum:

Bibliografische Information der Deutschen
Nationalbibliothek: Die Deutsche
Nationalbibliothek verzeichnet diese Publikation in
der Deutschen Nationalbibliografie; detaillierte
bibliografische Daten sind im Internet über
www.dnb.de abrufbar.

© 2020 Peter Oberfrank – Hunziker
Herstellung und Verlag
BoD – Books on Demand, Norderstedt

ISBN 9783751901987

nature colourful is ever celebrating
good sport and NHL jerseys in many
colours and accurate colours in nature
with wonderful being and enjoying .....
remembering ewigi Big Love wedding
in white curch from me Peter and
Michelle and Peter was giving Michelle
as wedding flower a unique Lichelle
and also remembering flower partying
and confettis and NHL playing and
celebrating NHL Stanley Cup trophies
nhli and red heart Trophy and NHL
stanley Cup trophies NHL happy unique
ever and NHL ever wedding and NHL
Sport ever and deep is blue ..... dark
blue is celebrating all ....

unique is ever and with memories and beautiful being ….. all is in heart and thinking and doing and enjoying and joyfulling …..

rosa church in Pensylvania

green church in asianti

white black marmori church in Rome

grey church in London Buckingham palace region

black church in multicoloursstyle in St. Louis

church Rapperswil with my home in Miami

coloured church St. Pauls Cathedral in
New York and also my homi

church Doha

church St. Stephansdom in Vienna in Austria

chicago churchi american indian

american church in Boston

flower church in Los Angeles

gardening church in Nashville

church sandburgi at the beach in
Montreal

.

church towering in Toronto

easy church in Madrid

high woody church in Barcelona

christmas tree church in Paris

church journeying in marmorstahl style

church in castleing style in San Francisco

church dschungeling in Brasilia

church iceiglustyling in nordpol city

church hütteli in südpol towni

church naturefestival zurundu in africa
metropoli town

church hostelling in Dubai

church halling in asiano

church Kölner Dome

church Homburg Domkuppeln

church great roofing in asian

church tentiandi in Tokyo

church culun in Zürich

church atztekondo in Mexiko

church lirondolo in amazonien

church buntondo in africancitylo

church high clifting in Ottawa

church rounding in Vancouver

church eyundo in Minnesota

church holzundo in Nashville nature
region

church washundolo in Washington

church tampalundindo in Tampa bay
lightning city

church in naturewood styling daliando
in Dallas

church flowerundoinu in Kairo in Egypt

church natureever in Region Germany

church indianying